THE KNOPF POETRY SERIES

Skating with Heather Grace

Skating with Heather Grace

Thomas Lynch

Alfred A. Knopf 1986 New York

THIS IS A BORZOI BOOK
PUBLISHED BY ALFRED A. KNOPF, INC.

COPYRIGHT © 1986 BY THOMAS LYNCH

ALL RIGHTS RESERVED UNDER INTERNATIONAL AND PAN-AMERICAN
COPYRIGHT CONVENTIONS. PUBLISHED IN THE
UNITED STATES BY ALFRED A. KNOPF, INC., NEW YORK,
AND SIMULTANEOUSLY IN CANADA BY
RANDOM HOUSE OF CANADA LIMITED, TORONTO.
DISTRIBUTED BY RANDOM HOUSE, INC., NEW YORK.

LIBRARY OF CONGRESS CATALOGING-IN-PUBLICATION DATA

LYNCH, THOMAS.
SKATING WITH HEATHER GRACE.
√ (KNOPF POETRY SERIES ; #24)
I. TITLE.
PS3562.Y43785   1986   811'.54   86–45299
ISBN 0–394–55480–9
ISBN 0–394–74756–9 (PBK.)

SOME POEMS IN THIS WORK WERE ORIGINALLY PUBLISHED
IN THE FOLLOWING PUBLICATIONS, TO WHOSE EDITORS
THE AUTHOR EXPRESSES HIS THANKS:
ADRIFT, ANN ARBOR MAGAZINE, BOSTON REVIEW, THE CHOUTEAU REVIEW,
COLORADO-NORTH REVIEW, CYPHERS, THE GREAT LAKES REVIEW,
THE HIRAM POETRY REVIEW, MID AMERICAN REVIEW,
THE MIDWEST QUARTERLY, MSS, AND THE POETRY IRELAND REVIEW.
"LEARNING GRAVITY" WAS ORIGINALLY PUBLISHED IN
THE AGNI REVIEW. "MARRIAGE," AND "WINTERKILL"
WERE ORIGINALLY PUBLISHED IN QUARTERLY WEST.
"A DEATH," "THE OLD DILEMMA," "A DOG WITH CHARACTER,"
"THE WIDOW," AND "THE GRANDMOTHERS" WERE
ORIGINALLY PUBLISHED IN POETRY.

MANUFACTURED IN THE UNITED STATES OF AMERICA

FIRST EDITION

FOR ROSE AND EDDIE
AND
MY CHILDREN

Moveen is a townland on the west coast of Ireland situated in County Clare, on the peninsula that forms the upper lip of the mouth of the River Shannon. It is where my people come from and where my cousin Nora Lynch still lives, now in her eighties. Her brother, Tommy Lynch, died in the spring of 1971, and is buried in the graveyard at Moyarta, just south of Moveen, near the estuarial town of Carrigaholt. I first visited these places in the winter and spring of 1970 and have returned many times since.

Mercywood is the name of the sanitarium in Ann Arbor, Michigan, to which Roethke was taken after bouts of manic-depression. The treatment of choice in those days was hydrotherapy. Certain lines in the ninth section of "Learning Gravity" are Roethke's, including "Love begets love" and "I watch the river wind itself away" from "The Motion" in *The Far Field*. From the same poem, "Knowing how all things alter in the seed" became, in mine, "Who knows how all things alter in the seed?"

T L

Skating with Heather Grace

Michael's Reply to the White Man

Listen, mister! I'm not one of those
who feels prenatal in the tub or has some
trauma in his childhood to account
for what it is that dogs me now. I do
no drugs or booze except the sociables
to blow the wondrous coals in me to flame
to where I sing songs, talk in tongues, fix names
to hitherto unknown things. Syllables
are the things I do, and do them carefully
so the great-grandkids of folks like you
will have something from this dire century
besides Freud and wars and hula-hoops.
See, what I'm really after is that tune
God hummed that Monday when he made the world.
What's more, I get paid for it, and pretty good—
unlike my ancient cousin, Mahon "The Crazed."
If you're still after something in my blood,
the blood is his, that wild man's, who raved
up and back the tribal holds of Munster
lamenting the piddling stipend paid to bards,
rhyming in favor of a living wage
for them that lived by rhyming. He was pure outrage.
Which didn't much endear him to his liege lord
who'd no use for those ungrateful hexameters
and might've had poor Mahon's tongue removed,
but it was Ireland, and centuries ago,
and a poet's foibles were pretty much approved
because, though daft, he kept the Histories alive
of kings and cattle raids and their comely wives.
So Mahon was left, more or less, alone.
Which is all I wanted, to be left alone.

And to get some good sleep because I'm bone-
tired of the pace I've had to keep up
day long and all night now for days. See, what
I really need is to get my body and my soul
aligned again with certain kindly stars,
rest and prayer, and after that a few jars
down at McCarthy's and then to hold
my wife in ways that are none of your business.
Actually, mine's a rather fit condition
despite the frenzied notes you're writing down.
I've nothing three months in the Knockmealdowns
with the Mrs. wouldn't cure, but Blue Cross is
ill-disposed to pay for that. But mark my words!
I resent your chemicals and diagnoses
and I'm maniac enough to pull a pox
down on the lot of you from the violent ward
upstairs where I have friends—the Halt and Lame
and Cherubim and Seraphim and Archangels.
And I want my belt back, and a change of socks
and a clean shave and my walking papers
with some admission of the mess you've made
in my case and cab fare for the ride home.
Or else I'll do what Mahon would have done.
I'll fire up a baleful Blood Curse poem
to dry the very seed inside you. Once
he wrecked some sniveling Brit who stiffed him
for a wedding song. Old Mahon turned that awful baritone
against the man, who ran off barking or turned to stone.
In all the versions of it, no one missed him.

A Death

In the end you want the clean dimensions of it mentioned;
to know the thing adverbially—*while asleep,*
after long illness, tragically in a blaze—

as you would the word of any local weather:
where it gathered, when it got here, how it kept
the traffic at a standstill, slowed the pace,

closed the terminals. Lineage & Issue, Names & Dates—
the facts you gain most confidence in facing—
histories and habitats and whereabouts.

Speak of it, if you speak of it at all, in parts.
The C.V.A. or insufficiency or growth
that grew indifferent to prayer and medication.

Better a tidy science for a heart that stops
than the round and witless horror of someone who
one dry night in perfect humor ceases measurably to be.

The Sin-Eater

Argyle the sin-eater came the day after—
a narrow hungry man whose laughter
and the wicked upturn of his one eyebrow
put the local folks in mind of trouble.
But still they sent for him and sat him down
amid their whispering contempts to make
his table near the dead man's middle,
and brought him soda bread and bowls of beer
and candles which he lit against the reek
that rose off that impenitent cadaver
though bound in skins and soaked in rosewater.
Argyle eased the warm loaf right and left
and downed swift gulps of beer and venial sin
then lit into the bread now leavened with
the corpse's cardinal mischiefs; then he said
"Six pence, I'm sorry." And the widow paid him.
Argyle took his leave then, down the land
between hay-reeks and Shorthorns with their calves
considering the innocence in all
God's manifold Creation but for Man;
and how he'd perish but for sin and mourning.
Two parishes between here and the ocean.
A bellyful tonight is what he thought,
please God, and breakfast in the morning.

Venice

My wife undressing in the moonlight sleeve by sleeve.
Late duty with our croupy middle son
she got to breathe by coaxing medicine
and VapoRub and steam. She yawns and leaves
the door ajar for closer listening.
Here is how affection settles in. You dream
a girl you had in Venice years ago
off-season, and a room with long windows
so the light she stood in nakedly
danced as the breeze danced in the drapery—
her skin awash in ivory and shadows.
Outside the vaporetti bubble in the water—
late boats to the Lido and the Zattere.
Down the hall a boy turns in his sleep.

The Blood We Paid For

Our old dog, long into his dotage, yawns—
a half-blind version of a breed that bred
among the Celts and kept their women clean
by barking off the covetous among their kind
when the husbands had gone off pillaging,
making poems and chaos in the next county.

Later, when the Celts themselves had settled in
and took to one god and wearing collars,
their dogs grew tame and even-tempered, tending
sheep and living to a good age; slept for hours
the way our own dog, sprawled on the linoleum,
listens to the breeze sing underneath

the door we never weatherstripped and hears
in some corpuscle of his ancient blood
the rage of wind matting his wet fur back,
sending a lather up from the seawrack
to float among the sea birds, hears them screech
above a band of wild men half-blind with drink,

who, having brought their plunder to the land's end,
ready their flimsy boats along the beach.
It was, of course, the blood we paid for. Spent
good money in bad times for a pedigree—
a hundred dollars, fifteen years ago
for what my wife claimed was a dog with character.

Nor will she let me, much as I'm inclined
(watching the pearlescent cataract
bloom in his good eye) when he's wholly blind,
coax him toward a stand of trees out back
and, because we've both grown overcivilized,
murder him with utmost dignity.

The West Window in Moveen

From here my great-grandfather stood and looked out
over the heather and blackthorn ditches
upland to Newtown where the evening moved
among the lamplit vigils of his countrymen,
each of them busy with their beads or votives,
snug in their rentals for the time being.
There was ever a wind off the ocean;
ever the prospect of rain for the haying;
ever the landlord and priest and the Mrs.,
children and Friesians. He kept praying
for a signal of Divine Intention—
a voice or a vision or a holy dream
of grand living in Jackson, Michigan,
his sons with the flattened speech of Yankees,
desk jobs and dollars and early pensions.
On the best nights he would look to the southwest
over the Shannon where the Kerry hills
grew mountainous and could only imagine
the primal lives of anchorites in stone
whose holy fever forced them ever westward
to the rock cliffs of Dingle, Skelligs, and Blaskets
half-crazed from their fasts and abstinence,
willing as the sea birds or the mackerel shoals.
Maybe it was the quiet or the dark
or dreamless sleep that sent him from the land
out of Moveen with his tin footlocker—
three weeks at sea in a cheerless steerage
with Mike and Tommy, the priest I'd be named for,
and Brigid, the Mrs., who was big that time—
fat with the makings of my grandfather.

With Tapers Quenched

I was nearly sound. Unaccountably
those blue acoustics rose in me as I rose
half-dreaming still that old dream of Lago
di Auronzo, that year in Italy,
our August in the Dolomites. I was
the bright blue hum of the sky that day
and under it, the whisper of bird wings,
and under them, where boatfuls of lovers
were tracing lazy ovals on the lake,
I was the oar's curl and the song the heart sings
and the hush between them as he leans to kiss
her ever so lightly on the eyelids.
Later that evening I was the slow hiss
the light's immersion made in the water.

A Family of Fishermen

In all his dreams of death it was his heart that failed him.
It ran in the family like bellies and tempers
and though his mother's people favored the long pull
and died mostly of kidneys or pneumonias,
skinny and bewildered in their nineties, all
the men drank whiskey and died of big hearts,
huffing and puffing to their purple ends.
So he held to his history and was ever ready
for one bolt out of nowhere that would lay him low
with only the juice left for one last wisdom,
maybe: *I always loved you* or *I told you so*
or *I must be dreaming*. He must have dreamt
a hundred times of how his great-great-grandfather
after a half day's fishing the cliffs at Doonlickey
could feed the whole parish on pollack and mackerel
till one day somehow he turned up missing
and washed up later in the bay at Goleen
wrapped up in his tackle of ribbons and sinkers
and made, in spite of it, a lovely summer corpse.
So he lit out in the pitch dark with the same instincts,
crossing the winter of his lake to where
he banged at the bare ice till his heart was breaking,
because of beauty, because the cold stars seemed
the blank eyes of women he had always loved,
and he told them so and thought he must be dreaming
to see his family, a family of fishermen,
approaching as the day broke under snowfall, so
he lay down in the first few inches of it.

Tatyana

Now I've forgotten what you looked like naked.
Dry grief to wonder were the nipples brown,
the breasts so small, or how
the flesh and filigree of bones embraced
in all those postures of your love.
I remember saying once how fine it was
to work a sweat up with you. Then I said
no two get closer than we do at this—
this fretful linkage between bodies.
I made that up of course. I was
frightened and cocksure and might've believed it.
The skin's intelligence, I thought.
Glad tuition of the flesh.
Intimate knowledge of another.
We were, neither of us, certain.
Now we are old friends. We meet for drinks.
The talk is cautious and well-read,
affecting ignorance and equilibrium.
Sometimes I think I can see you laid bare again.
I think I see you naked when your eyes
turn aimlessly beyond our conversation
into the air where we make our visit and where
nothing ever happens. Nothing has.

Like My Father Waking Early

Even for an undertaker, it was odd.
My father always listened through the dark,
half-dreaming hours to a radio
that only played police and fire tunes.
Mornings, he was all the news of break-ins, hold-ups,
now and then a house gone up in flames
or a class of disorder he'd call, frowning,
a *Domestic*. They were dying in our sleep.
My father would sit with his coffee and disasters,
smoking his Luckies, reading the obits.
"I've buried boys who played with matches
or swam alone or chased balls into streets
or ate the candy that a stranger gave them . . ."
or so he told us as a form of caution.
When I grew older, the boys he buried toyed
with guns or drugs or drink or drove too fast
or ran with the wrong crowd headlong into peril.
One poor client hung himself from a basement rafter—
heartsick, as my father told it, for a girl.
By sixteen, I assisted with the bodies,
preparing them for burial in ways
that kept my dread of what had happened to them busy
with arteries and veins and chemistries—
a safe and scientific cousin, once removed
from the horror of movements they never made.
Nowadays I bury children on my own.
Last week two six-year-olds went through the ice
and bobbed up downstream where the river bends
through gravel and shallows too fast to freeze.
We have crib deaths and cancers, suicides,
deaths in fires, deaths in cars run into trees,

and now I understand my father better.
I've seen the size of graves the sexton digs
to bury futures in, to bury children.
Upstairs, my children thrive inside their sleep.
Downstairs, I'm tuning in the radio.
I do this like my father, waking early,
I have my coffee, cigarettes and worry.

Marriage

He wanted a dry mouth, whiskey and warm flesh
and for all his bothersome senses to be still.
He let his eyeballs roll back in their sockets until
there was only darkness. He grew unmindful
of the spray of moonwash that hung in the curtains,
the dry breath of the furnace, parts of a tune
he'd hummed to himself all day. Any noise
that kept him from his own voice hushed.
He wanted to approximate the effort of snowdrift,
to gain that sweet position over her repose
that always signaled to her he meant business,
that turned them into endless lapping dunes.
He wanted her mouth to fill like a bowl with vowels,
prime and whole and indivisible, O . . . O . . . O . . .

Lessons from Berkeley

Dualco, Dualco . . . Why do we bother
to figure and refigure these old formulae?
What can it matter if
knowing these grand axioms binds us no less?
The Laws of Life: We breathe
or blink, say, twenty times a minute.
Twice in a good month we have dreams
of sweet delirium. Once
every ten years, more or less,
a heartbreak or some big luck in the lottery.
One birth, one death, a marriage and a half, one
in between. Between the two of us
my brains are sore from it.
Let God keep watch tonight and listen for
the tree falling in the forest,
all that well-kept, secret, human noise
of new birth, lovers, and the nearly dead,
any distant smack or boom or bleat
by hearing which He earns His endless keep.
Esse est percipere, Dualco—
To be etc., etc.
Let's you and me go out and drink to excess as
if it were required of our kind
to blight our senses now and then, get blind
and willing and benign,
like particles of some vast perception:
the rock and wave and all unfeeling things
that outlive by a longshot
things that think or see or sense,
articles of their own impermanence.

O Canada

Some nights he'd watch hockey and so she'd rock
with a novel or her Valéry and go to France
where she and several guests of the gay prince
picnic and play at croquet on the château grounds.
Lace and ribbons are all the fashion rage
and ladies in chiffon and high coiffures
fan their bright bosoms like birds of song.
And there are men with names like pink flowers
or instruments of sound in silk stockings
and plump satin breeches to knee length who seem fond
of dabbing their rouged lips with handkerchiefs
they keep in their coat sleeves for such occasions
while all around their wigs hum yellow honeybees,
drawn to their powders and colognes and toiletries.
And she is out among them. And her hand is kissed
by gentlemen of rank and her opinion sought
on Couperin and Molière and Poussin—
all high etiquette and courtly talk.
Out in the garden, she hears the gardener sing,
between hedgerows of juniper and yew,
O Canada, our home and native land. He moves
by evening light through his green diocese,
smelling of dung and mulch and growing things,
heartsick for that hard country of his youth.
Some nights he'd take her to his room upstairs
and speak in that far dialect she loved
of ice and earth and qualities of air—

his True North, strong and free, O Canada;
and then he'd make hardbody love to her.
Next morning she'd make omelettes and he'd thumb
the newspaper for word of Guy Lafleur
or Marcel Dionne. And she'd be pleased because
that was the style of the country he'd come from.

Argyle in Agony

Some sins Argyle couldn't stomach much.
Sins against virgin girls and animals,
women bearing children, men gone blind
from all but self-abusive reasons gave him
stomach troubles, like over-seasoned meat
he oughtn't to have eaten, but he always did.
Some nights those evils woke him in his sleep—
gaseous and flatulent, bent over his puke bowl,
resolved again to draw the line somewhere,
to leave the dirty work to younger men
or anyway, to up his prices.
Maybe steady work with nuns whose vices
were rumored to go down like tapioca.
But no, those clever ladies lived forever
and for all their charities would starve the man
who counted for his feed on their transgressions.
Better to go on as he always had,
eating sins and giving souls their blessed rest.
What matter that his innards heaved against
a steady diet of iniquities
or that children worked their mayhem on his head
by carving pumpkins up in fearful effigies?
He had his holy orders and his mission.
He had the extreme unction of his daily bread.

The Widow

Her life was spent in deference to his comfort.
The rocking chair was his, the window seat,
the firm side of the mattress.

Hers were the midnights with sickly children,
pickups after guests left, the single
misery of childbirth. She had duties:

to feed him and to follow and to forgive his few
excesses. Sometimes he drank, he puffed cigars,
he belched, he brought the money in

and brought Belleek and Waterford for birthdays,
rings and rare scents for Christmas; twice he sent
a card with flowers: "All my love, always."

At night she spread herself like linen out
for him to take his feastly pleasures in
and liked it well enough, or said she did, day in,

day out. For thirty years they agreed on this
until one night, after dinner dancing,
he died a gassy death at fifty—turned

a quiet purple in his chair, quit breathing.
She grieved for him with a real grief for she missed him
sorely. After six months of this, she felt relieved.

Rotary International

There I am with the scholarship winners.
On my right is the girl with the 3.8's
who's going into Nursing. Next to her
in the short sleeves there is Clifford Shore,
our superintendent of schools. He chose these two
from a list of twenty-odd and said they all
had merit. That poxy fellow with the smile
is sincere about his biochemistry and plans
a future in molecular recovery.
On the end, poor Clayton Stone, a Rotarian
who put the money up in loving memory of
his wife, who died last year, December 10.
My left hand, with the scrimshaw cufflink
you can see, tenders the check to her
while my right hand, which you do not see,
at the suggestion of the photographer,
is around her waist. My fingertips
are eased into the space between her
first and second ribs, which accounts
in part for all the smiles you can see.
What I'm thinking there, invisibly, is we
could take the prize and spend it all on planes
and good hotels and room service and her
education and be back here in a week.
Behind us is the Sunny Side Cafe.

The luncheon special you can see that day
was BLT's. The only other thing
you cannot see is how we wished them luck
and then agreed to meet down at Irene's
for soup and sandwiches and drinks
to toast ourselves, the three of us,
Cliff and Clay and me, on a job well done.

A Dream of Death
in the First-Person

I'm coming the coast road into Moveen.
This part replays itself, over and over
to a standstill, until I'm hardly moving.
Out in the ocean are islands I've never
noticed in pictures I have of that place.
I take this as a signal I'm dreaming.
Within the dream, then, I begin to bless
myself against such peril as these dreams
in all their early versions put me in.
In one, great soaring gulls keep coaxing me,
by angles of their flight I understand,
to join them in the air beyond the land
and make my life with them diving between islands.

Skating with Heather Grace

Apart from the apparent values,
there are lessons in the circular:
paradigms for history,
time in a round world, turning,
love with another of your species—

To watch my only daughter
widening her circles is to ease
headlong into the traffic
of her upbringing.

Until nearly four she screamed
at my absence, mourned
my going out for any reason,
cried at scoldings,
agreed to common lies regarding
thunder, Christmas,
baby teeth. Last year

she started school
without incident;
this year ballet and new math. Soon

I think my love will seem
entirely deficient.

Later there's the hokey-pokey
and dim lights for the partners' dance.
She finds a shaky nine-year-old
to skate around
in counter-clockwise orbits,
laughing.

Is it more willingness than balance?
Is letting go the thing that keeps her steady?

I lean against the sideboards sipping
coffee. I keep a smile ready.

Learning Gravity

Here is how it happens. One soft night
you're sitting in an outdoor bar with friends,
glad for the long days and your own survival,
which has come for the time being to depend
upon what conversation you can make
out of Beethoven or the cinema,
out of the way the loss of light proceeds
from top to bottom in the sky, always
abiding by those few sure-footed laws
whereby things rise and fall, arrive and take
their leave according to their gravity—
earthbound, in balance, timely and at ease.
When who shows up among the tabletops
but somebody you haven't seen in years.
You follow him into another room
and find him staring in a wall of mirrors.
He doesn't know how long it's been or what
he's done. He has no plans, he says, except
to be gone tomorrow. Much later, on
account of this, you will begin to grieve.

That time in Moveen, the sky became
so full of motion the soft air seemed
too quick a thing to breathe in, so I sang

out where the gulls glide on the edge of weather
songs in praise of rootlessness and wayfare
and wore my newfound whereabouts with honor

the way a man does who goes traveling
without a war on or a famine:
c/o third cousins, West Clare, Ireland.

My Love, I wrote home in a letter, here
the old arrangement of the rock & water
gathers up the coastline in a lather.

The slate cliffs lean with the weight of land
into the heft & heave of ocean.
I watch the tide fall and rise and fall again.

I thought of you then as a secret in the water
that made waves out of the elements of order
and taught them surge and swell and billow

so the air filled with a rich noise below
the tall ledge of land I edged along
dizzy with the sweet enticement of the fall.

Kennedy had been dead by then for years.
My fall from innocence
began with a still frame from Zapruder's film—
a blurry likeness of the way he leaned
into his wife's hug with the look of damage,
and how she cuddled him as if he were
a bingy drunk who only liquored up
for holidays or funerals or for fun.
I thought, how much she loves him,

how surely dead he seems. Since then
I measure my departure from where I was
that day, in Christian Brothers' School
and the flat voice on the p.a. saying
all that we could do was pray.
I put you with the nuns, next door, that day—
your life in those times parallel with mine,
arranged by height or alphabet for sacraments.
First Communion, Confirmation,
the Death of Presidents.

I remember my poor cousin in his bed.
A quiet replica of calm,
his mouth propped shut with his daily missal.
A rosary kept his hands crossed on his chest.
Inside the women hummed their beads and sipped
sweet wine and ripe Cidona. In the yard
the men complained of prices and the spring that left
a mudwreck of their fields and kept their cows in.
"The Lord've mercy on him, Tommy was
a daycent man he was and innocent.
A pure St. Francis with his cattle, shy
when it came to women or the drink.
Sure Faith, there was no speck of sin in him."
And then in deference to his Yankee namesake,
bloodshot from the porter or the grief,
they brought their hopeless talk around to Kennedy.

His was the first death in our lives that took.
Until then our heroes were invincible:

the cartoon cat who swallows dynamite,
the cowpoke who turns up in a rodeo
after getting murdered in a barfight.
That was the apple we bit for truth:
the permanence of death for him, for us
the death of permanence. For days
we watched him go the way of the
Friday Meat Rule and the Latin Mass,
the rhythm method, black and white TV,
true love and romance, our favorite saints,
Cardinal Sins, Contrary Virtues, all
parts of life we'd made a part of us that changed.
O Jack, here twenty years since then
we only think of you as dead.

Your pink notes came up the coast road with the postman.
Word about friends, weddings and the spring

in Michigan, and Roethke, whose growth of poems
you'd grown enamored of. "He sings and sings

root tunes and seed songs, hums the fern and foliage."
Of course, he'd learned the lesson in his garden—

how one day getting on to Autumn
you come across hard knowledge like a corpse

left out in the dull light by some passion,
murderous or accidental, nonetheless

passion of a human sort. You appraise the body's beauty:
a leptosome among the leaves. The rare lines

of the ribs poke out beneath the skin
like kite-work of some former elegance. The leaves rise on

the small ground wind. The birdlike beauty lies
solid in its lack of movement, quiet as the moon is,

drinking the darkness like the moon does, turning
damp and fertile. Going to seed.

With this intelligence you begin, then,
thick with excitement and new fright.

I remember the bones of my kinsmen,
long since dead, unearthed again in the grave's
reopening—femurs and half-skulls and ribs
in piles at graveside at Moyarta.
And the general reverence of townsmen,
neighbors, thick countrymen from the creamery
or local bog, thatchers and fishermen,
all of whom had doings with our newly dead.
All of whom had come to their consensus
after mass in boozy In Memoriams:
"An honest airy man he was. By cripes,
the saint of the peninsula! A far,
far better specimen than the likes of us."
When the priest said so, we made for Moyarta,

shouldering the saint of that peninsula
into the hilly middle ground between
the River Shannon's mouth and the North Atlantic.

Consider Roethke in his tub at Mercywood,
crazy with his glad mayhem, how he would
soak for hours like a length of bogwood

lolling and bobbing in the water.
I think of you, your body in the water
and how the light glistened in the beads of water

that ran down between your breasts like islands
among the bare geographies I learned
the year that we were lovers, after Ireland.

Who knows how all things alter in the seed?
From shoot to stem to full bloom then to seed,
clumsy with their own invention until they see

that everything that breathes requires death.
A fierce affection is a thing like death.
Love begets love, then life, then death.

I watch the river wind itself away,
delighted at your bright flesh drying, at the way
the earthly body learns its earthly ways.

1948–Expect from birth
68.6 years, give or take.
A useful figure for, say, figuring
career options, life goals, middle age,
with further applications in the abstract:
to arrive at what to expect from death, subtract
the Useful Figure from Infinity.
The Crude Death Rate for 1963 was
nine point four per thousand, which includes
infant mortality, less the fetal deaths,
a poet, Roethke, and a President.
1970–some notable variants:
bad flu in the Middle West,
the same war in Asia, always
pestilence in the usual places.
The remarkable number: 100%.

I'm the one who keeps a rough count of the dead.
I count whatever's unclaimed after months
of reasonable inquiries, want ads, word of mouth—
things get around once word gets out.
It's a small place we live in, after all.
Which explains the recent interest in your case.
Because it seems you've come into your strength
so that you fall no faster than thirty-two
feet per second per second and you move
always in accordance with the rules of life
that govern bodies moving in the realm of light.
What is it you keep faith in, hope for,
count your blessings by? Life after death?

Death after life? After sex a cigarette?
Why is it I have come to think of you without
a history or vision or the dreadful tow
of things that moved us and the way we went
out into the real world full of innocence,
passion, and mortality? I don't know.
But things happen every day here.
We could all be alive tomorrow.

Sometimes I come here for a drink with friends.
Sometimes I drink too much and feel like crying
God, God! I'm a sad man with a thin heart dying
from complications of a complex race of men
who all their lives look for holes to fill
with all their lives. Their lives and loss of will.

A Clearing in the Woods

You have come into a clearing in the woods
and want to live your life out, here, alone,
joyous and remote among the catbirds

letting the light fall on you and the shade
in hourly changing angles as a grace
endlessly descending among tree limbs

while growing in you is the will to grow
mindless of the niggling everyday
profusion of detail by which you know

uselessly the names and dates and shape of things.
After a while, you will begin to sing.
Harmless and plentiful you make the sounds.

Bent on nothing that does not bend with ease
you and your song rise in the leafy air
chancy as bass spawn in a mallard's underwings.

A Note on the Rapture
to His True Love

A blue bowl on the table in the dining room
fills with sunlight. From a sunlit room
I watch my neighbor's sugar maple turn
to shades of gold. It's late September. Soon . . .
Soon as I'm able I intend to turn
to gold myself. Somewhere I've read that soon
they'll have a formula for prime numbers
and once they do, the world's supposed to end
the way my neighbor always said it would—
in fire.   I'll bet we'll all be given numbers
divisible by One and by themselves
and told to stand in line the way you would
for prime cuts at the butcher's. In the end,
maybe it's every man for himself.
Maybe it's someone hollering All Hands On
Deck! Abandon Ship! Women and Children First!
Anyway, I'd like to get my hands on
you.   I'd like to kiss your eyelids and make love
as if it were our last time, or the first,
or else the one and only form of love
divisible by which I yet remain myself.
Mary, folks are disappearing one by one.
They turn to gold and vanish like the leaves
of sugar maples. But we can save ourselves.
We'll pick our own salvations, one by one,
from a blue bowl full of sunlight until none is left.

October

The brown season of putrefaction's on:
leaf-fall and bloodsport, upstream the fish
obeying an impulse to breed and finish,
spawn in the gravel, blacken in deep holes,
rot in the brush along the river's edge.
What do we learn from loss but how to lose?
This year I grieve for the salmon and the oak,
all game breeds and my own endangered soul
because it cannot take the fall the way it once could
and counts each death a portion of its own
and holds on only to the poorest class of hope.
Do we bag the leaves this year, or burn?

Pornography

My father had a *Bell's Pathology*.
He studied it in Mortuary School.
A thick pictorial of sicknesses
so grisly or disfiguring or rare.
There was a man whose one leg never grew,
in boxer shorts, a giant held a she-dwarf,
Siamese twins joined at the belly,
a hapless lady with a goiter
and foreign names for each my father englished as:
"As kids they hardly touched their vegetables."

Pat's dad kept a stack of magazines
hidden under stairs down to the basement.
Inside them, breathless shapes stretched out in satin—
like figurines in porcelain at rest,
and held their breath so that their breasts swelled
like rare new forms of intelligent life
and held our broad arousal with the way
a bent knee, a bit of lingerie,
or the edge of light itself, in those days,
hid from Pat and me their most illegal parts.

The Orient

He had sustained his share of treacheries
so that it came as no surprise when his
nerve went slack or the wife ignored him, when
his six-year-old brought home a surly note
about his listening skills or self-control.
For these he had outlined a stratagem.

First off he'd drink himself horizontal
against his sleeplessness and to induce
that dream he always dreamt in black and white
in which he was the calm and steely kind
who rode in a rickshaw full of counsel
and after whom the mission teachers ran

ripe in their kimonos and sweet breath as
mandarins in a wet month, for his songs.
Careful in closing always to arrange
the usual sunset into which he strode
off in the direction, he'd begin to hope,
of a place with clean toilets and a view.

The Liturgist

Pressing the linens for Thanksgiving, she
recalls the bright dress she married in—
tight lace and organdy; how after ironing
she held it to herself, arm over arm,
like a thin partner in a dance and danced
in slow approving turns around the room
like the morning of her first communion:
ready as she'd been for anything, ever—
for the first time with him, the mix of sweat
and sweet breath, fond percussion, how she pressed
beneath the low commotion of their lovemaking.
It seemed to her then like the care of linens
or the care of children, or in spring,
like pressing new seeds into her garden
or the meal she spreads out for Thanksgiving:
a portion chore, a portion sacrament.

I Felt Myself Turning

I felt myself turning, circling downward.
The shape of my descent put me in mind
of Yeats or tornadoes or the way sea birds,
focusing their hunger over baitfish shoals,
would fall in tightening spirals off the wind.
I kept trying to formulate a set of goals
or a plan on the off-chance it all would end
with my being offered one final chance
to make good, a last meal, or a cigarette.
There was comfort in those great gulls, how they bent
against their fatal gravity—at the last
moment turning up with fish, effortless
in their ascension, full of hope, they seemed
a new life form light-years removed from me.

A Good Death Even
When It Kills You

Afterwards, she watched the snowfall closely,
counting her blessings from a window indoors,
where only the low din of tableware
and hushed neighbors among the casseroles
trespassed her focus on the ghost-white weather.
Anyway, he was doing what he liked most—
out before daylight with his shanty and lanterns,
wax-worms and jig poles, thermos and brandy;
the whole lashup in long tow on foot to where
last night his calculations put a school of bluegill—
instead of hooked to some intensive hardware
to chart and graph and lengthen the whole thing,
or long suffering to the same end with a cancer
or half a dozen other ways she knew of. No,
this was a quick and lethal one, according
to the coroner. And she was glad for him.
A good death, even when it kills you, is
nonetheless some better than a bad one.
When the snow quit falling, there was still the lake
and then a stubble of cornfield uphill in rows
and then two birds above a stand of winter oaks
circling in the gray unfocused space of weather.
When she could see no farther, she began to hate him
for fifteen years of rearing children and
for cold nights when she warmed against him and for
all the tender habits he observed in love, because
he was all she'd ever wanted and was dead at forty,
spudding the ice for a hole, to get a line in.

To Her Sisters on the
Nature of the Universe

I think of all landscapes as feminine
and of the many seasons as a man
whose weather is the ever-changing reason
he will give for wanting you. As for hands,
I think of them as daybreak and nightfall
hourly easing over my skin. My skin
is the morning you awaken to snowfall
drifting to berms and swells and shallowings
like tidal oceans overtaking land.
I think of oceans as the way a man
returns to me from exile or wars,
blood-drunk and frightened to the bone. Of course
he hears her then, asleep between my breasts—
the angel charged with beckoning the dead;
and wakes up gladsome for the soft iambic code
my pulse assures him with: Not yet, not yet.

Where It Came From

Where it came from if it came from anywhere
was the deep pit within him where his anger was
hunched like a bad beast back on its haunches
ready to hunker up whenever he got ready
whenever he'd had enough of this or when
love turned sour left him out of love.

Trouble was whenever he got troubled
by something lesser men got lessened by
or needled by some needless hurt or
thought of some lost intimate he only thought
Good God! Might all this come to some last good
to ease the ache I've grown lately accustomed to?

Furthermore he seemed to draw no further
comfort from those things he once drew comfort
from: Ease of wit and easy motion from
one good hideout to another. Once
when he was at his peak of loneliness he went
nowhere for a good long while where he wasn't known.

Noon on Saturday

I

The fire whistle sets the dogs to howling,
adding their odd song to the sound of damage,
and everywhere folks seem to carry on
like nothing has happened. And nothing has.
No emergency. It's noon on Saturday.
Most Saturdays at noon I sit like this,
a thankless member of my subspecies,
at odds with all the elements of grace—
the wife and kids, the furnace kicking on—
able to manage only this much faith:
Life goes on. I say this to myself. Life goes on.
I rummage in the house for signs of loss.

II

I watch the winter out the window gathering.
White where the ground was, gray where the sky was,
a company of blackbirds in a walnut tree
holding forth, no doubt, about the weather:
The winter, you say, will be long and cold.
The frost will deepen in the earth, the light
grow shorter till there seems no light at all.
O to have the bird's life in the air, to roll
on the air above the worst of weather,
to say I saw the whole thing from the sky—
the way the cold comes this time most years,
the same way as the darkness, and our flight.

III

Same as the way I'm inclined to sit here
hour after hour because my life
seems oddly affected by the weather,
by the sight of cold birds in a bald tree
grieving the winter, figuring a way out.
When all I ever needed for a little warmth
was to pay the gas man and the ones I love
or to sing the same song over and over
because the sound it makes keeps me intact
like the one long note that signals danger,
proclaims a fire or a cardiac
out in the township or noon on Saturday.

A Woman with a Woman's Parts

If I think of you,
a woman with a woman's parts,
apart somehow from
all your other lives.
If I consider only private parts—
the bird throb in the throat
or rise and fall
of small breasts measuring the air
or the bare neck taut
in its white laughter,
the skin's dampness after
passion, the cheek's flush,
the eyelid's blue, the brief limbs'
stillness after lovemaking.
If I think of you,
a woman with a woman's parts,
and all the tidal powers of your sex.
O the awful genius of the heart.
The perfect memory of the flesh.

Wormwood

The one who took a pistol in his teeth
and blew his brains across the family room
and how his wife, for weeks, found little pieces
of his skull wedged in the wormwood paneling
as tokens of his longstanding discontent
provides a body for my deadly sentiment.
Or what about the one who lay between
his Buick's dual exhausts and breathed and breathed
until he was out of breath and at a loss
to say exactly what it was that went wrong.
There were, of course, the usual theories.

Argyle in Vapors

Vaporous and sore at heart, Argyle stood
in his doorway looking out at nothing.
The wind blew through him as if he wasn't.
As if he were, himself, a door ajar
through which one had to go to get nowhere
and wanting to go nowhere, there he stood—
a spectacle of shortfall and desire.
And all the voice of reason in him reasoned was
"Take heart, Argyle! This is seasonal.
The winter is a cruel but equal cross
borne only by the living in the name of Christ,
and though a cold encumbrance on the soul afire
with ministry and purpose, bear in mind
the dead will keep for days in such weather
and any climate so kind to a corpse
will shorten purgatory for those left alive
to huddle in their mud and wattles for some warmth."
Such comfort as that gave him helped him weather
well enough the chill and shortened days,
the noise of rats wintering in his thatch,
the endless bitter merriment at wakes.
By dark he dreamed the touch of female flesh—
all night in sweats and brimming scenes of pleasure
and waking up alone, he blamed the weather.

Pruning

She wonders do they feel
the loss of limbs as we do,
bristling in the air like haloes
over picture saints,
the prickly heat beyond
the stump's thick suturing,
the phantom hollering downstairs
for towels or clean socks,
shampoo or shaving cream.
Last year he did the
lilac and mock orange himself,
in June. He stood in the kitchen
sun-brown and penitent and said
an early cutting makes
somehow for better blooms.
At night she holds his pillow
to her ribs and rubs
carefully the rough edge of her wound.

The Grandmothers

A hundred sixty years of lucid memory sit
under a plump umbrella on the patio—
two widows nursing whiskey sours argue politics:

my grandmothers. When they turned eighty, we began
to mark their changes as we might a child's
in terms of sight, mobility and appetite,

teeth and toilet habits, clarity of speech,
a thousand calibers of round flight
by which my children make their distance now from me.

Sometimes I think of them as parts of me.
I think their ageless quarrels come to roost
like odd birds with an awkward plumage in my blood.

The one says tend your own twigs, peep and preen.
The other wings beyond the kindly orbit here
and sings, and sings, and sings.

The Student

What we had here was a brand of affliction
I'd read about in female magazines
for which candles and a good confession
were contraindicated. Shopping sprees,
new hairdos, a weekend in the Poconos
with a willing stranger were the well-known cures.
But I was broke and going bald and knew no
strangers. The thought I had was one of yours:
"I can talk myself into or out of
anything." You wrote that in a letter
years ago. And I began to wonder, was
it our own voices that failed us so badly
sometimes? The noise of our own souls that turned us
against the soft instructions of our dreams?

Woman Gardening

I want this to sound like a print from Monet,
to seem French and unfinished and best at a distance;
the blank little title to say it was
only an instant, without any history
or future, not part of a sequence
and need not be made into a movie.
So here is the garden's rock bordering
and the lilac bush she bends under
and how her hair falls correctly from the
blue barrettes, the packet of seeds in her back pocket,
and the small wrist making turns in the black dirt.
Her eyes and her lovers and the weather tomorrow
are not included here nor the names of the flowers
the seeds will turn into nor the secret
hosannas she sings nor the Easters
she dreams pressing seeds in her garden.

The Exhibitionist

I pull dull words out of the void and rub
the way a dry old man does stones
because he cannot race out with the waves and roll
like a dolphin rolling in the water
so walks the beach at first light in a haze
like waking in strange rooms the morning after
some rage or wind or passion has been spent—
bottles and odd shoes, blankets and towels,
the noise of gulls and bleach-white catfish bones.
He hunts among the litter for Petoskey stones.

And only wants to feel once in his skin again
the dire hold the sea puts on a man:
its half-embrace and half-repellency,
pulsing undertow and female gravity;
to hold his breath and come up glistening
and baptismal and full of mystery.
Full of whatever young men are full of
who row out past the sandbars after salmon
and row back when the moon's up with their limits,
to lie among their wives and womenkind and dream of fish.

A pointless pleasure only from the stones he finds.
He cleans and cuts and buffs and polishes
cufflinks and stickpins and curiosities,
to be spread out for the ladies at card parties,
for the VFW Women's Auxiliary,
or for powdery widows from the Eastern Star
who gasp politely at his exhibition,
allowing as how it must take up most nights.

For the Ex-Wife on the Occasion of Her Birthday

Let me say outright that I bear you no
unusual malice anymore. Nor
do I wish for you tumors or loose stools,
blood in your urine, oozings from any orifice.
The list is endless of those ills I do not pray befall you:
night sweats, occasional itching, PMS,
fits, starts, ticks, boils, bad vibes, vaginal odors,
emotional upheavals or hormonal disorders;
green discharges, lumps, growths, nor tell-tale signs of gray;
dry heaves, hiccups, heartbreaks, fallen ovaries
nor cramps—before, during, or after. I pray you only
laughter in the face of your mortality
and freedom from the ravages of middle age:
bummers, boredom, cellulite, toxic shock and pregnancies;
migraines, glandular problems, the growth of facial hair,
sagging breasts, bladder infections, menopausal rage,
flatulence or overdoses, hot flashes or constant nausea,
uterine collapse or loss of life or limb or faith
in the face of what might seem considerable debilities.
Think of your life not as half-spent but as half-full
of possibilities. The Arts maybe, or
Music, Modern Dance, or Hard Rock Videos.
Whatever, this is to say I hereby recant
all former bitterness and proffer only all the best
in the way of Happy Birthday wishes.
I no longer want your mother committed,
your friends banished, your donkey lovers taken out and shot
or spayed or dragged behind some Chevrolet of doom.
I pray you find that space or room or whatever it is
you and your shrink have always claimed you'd need
to spread your wings and realize your insuperable potential.

Godspeed is what I say, and good credentials:
what with your background in fashions and aerobics,
you'd make a fairly bouncy brain surgeon
or well-dressed astronaut or disc jockey.
The children and I will be watching with interest
and wouldn't mind a note from time to time
to say you've overcome all obstacles this time;
overcome your own half-hearted upbringing,
a skimpy wardrobe, your lowly self-esteem,
the oppression of women and dismal horoscopes;
overcome an overly dependent personality,
stretch marks, self-doubt, a bad appendix scar,
the best years of your life misspent on wifing and mothering.
So let us know exactly how you are once
you have triumphed, after all. Poised and ready
on the brink of, shall we say, your middle years,
send word when you have gained by the luck of the draw,
the kindness of strangers, or by dint of will itself
if not great fame then self-sufficiency.
Really, now that I've my hard-won riddance of you
signed and sealed and cooling on the books against
your banks and creditors; now that I no
longer need endure your whining discontent,
your daylong, nightlong carping over lost youth,
bum luck, spilt milk, what you might have been,
or pining not so quietly for a new life in
New York with new men; now that I have been
more or less officially relieved of
all those hapless duties husbanding
a woman of your disenchantments came to be,
I bid you No Deposits, No Returns,

but otherwise a very Happy Birthday.
And while this mayn't sound exactly like good will
in some important ways it could be worse.
The ancients in my family had a way with words
and overzealous habits of revenge
whereby the likes of you were turned to birds
and made to nest among the mounds of dung
that rose up in the wake of cattle herds
grazing their way across those bygone parishes
where all that ever came with age was wisdom.

How to Stay Alive

He found he had nothing of consequence
to say about the weather so he went
noiselessly about his sorry business—
a version of himself in which he kept
pace with his neighbors but at an arm's length
because his arms were too short and he ached
in ways he thought they'd hardly understand.
So he kept his distance, and assumed the stance
of someone he'd seen one time in a movie.

Damage

My own dilemma was not life but death.
I disapprove of hangings, pills, gas stoves,
gunplay, self-inflicted wounds with knives,
forks, spoons wielded in despair—here's the truth:
I'm frightened witless at the prospect of
some bomb or cancer out there with my name on it.
No, I'm no do-it-yourselfer, though I've
known a few who were and might half admit
a certain envy at their pure resolve,
the clarity of will which did themselves
such massive and irreparable damage.
After all the dust clears, I imagine
little difference—we, none of us survives
our awful will to live or will to die.

Argyle's Balance

Argyle kept his balance feeling himself
between two equal and opposing forces
each, at once, both fearsome and endearing.
He had dreams. In one a woman in her bright flesh
kneels in the river, bathing. Later, she
lies in the tall grass drying, reddening
her nipples with the juice of pomegranates,
offering them and her body to him.
This was his dream of youth and lovemaking,
of greensong, water, all life-giving things.
The other was a dream of himself, on his
deathbed. The children gather, dumbstruck
at his belly bulbous with flatus, fat
with the old sins of others and his own.
A priest stands ready with chrisms and forgiveness.
He always dreamt this after radishes.
These were the horizontal mysteries
from either one of which he would arise
breathless with intimacy and release,
envigored with deliverance, alive.
The answer he figured was to keep an arm's reach
between his waking self and either dream, listing
only slightly from upright anytime
the dreams made music and he would listen.

A NOTE ON THE TYPE

THIS BOOK WAS SET ON THE LINOTYPE IN JANSON,
A RECUTTING MADE DIRECT FROM TYPE CAST FROM
MATRICES LONG THOUGHT TO HAVE BEEN MADE BY
THE DUTCHMAN ANTON JANSON, WHO WAS A PRACTICING
TYPE FOUNDER IN LEIPZIG DURING THE YEARS
1668–1687. HOWEVER, IT HAS BEEN CONCLUSIVELY
DEMONSTRATED THAT THESE TYPES ARE ACTUALLY THE
WORK OF NICHOLAS KIS (1650–1702), A HUNGARIAN,
WHO MOST PROBABLY LEARNED HIS TRADE FROM THE
MASTER DUTCH TYPE FOUNDER DIRK VOSKENS.
THE TYPE IS AN EXCELLENT EXAMPLE OF THE
INFLUENTIAL AND STURDY DUTCH TYPES THAT
PREVAILED IN ENGLAND UP TO THE TIME
WILLIAM CASLON (1692–1766)
DEVELOPED HIS OWN
INCOMPARABLE DESIGNS FROM THEM.

COMPOSED, PRINTED AND BOUND BY
HERITAGE PRINTERS, INC.
CHARLOTTE, NORTH CAROLINA

TYPOGRAPHY AND BINDING DESIGN BY
TASHA HALL